Life in the THIRTEEN COLONIES

A VIEW OF THE TOWN OF BOSTON WITH SEVERAL SHIPS OF WAR IN THE HARBOUR.

Massachusetts

Deborah H. DeFord

children's press®
An imprint of
SCHOLASTIC

Library of Congress Cataloging-in-Publication Data

DeFord, Deborah H.
  Massachusetts / by Deborah H. DeFord.
    p. cm. — (Life in the thirteen colonies)
  Includes bibliographical references and index.
  ISBN 0-516-24572-4
  1. Massachusetts—History—Colonial period, ca. 1600-1775—Juvenile literature. 2. Massachusetts—History—1775-1865—Juvenile literature. I. Title. II. Series.
  F67.D36 2004
  974.4'02—dc22
                                    2004008873

1 2 3 4 5 6 7 8 9 10 R 13 12 11 10 09 08 07 06 05 04

A Creative Media Applications Production
Design: Fabia Wargin Design
Production: Alan Barnett, Inc.
Editor: Matt Levine
Copy Editor: Laurie Lieb
Proofreader: Tania Bissell
Content Research: Lauren Thogersen
Photo Researcher: Annette Cyr
Content Consultant: David Silverman, Ph.D.

CONTENTS

✳✳✳✳✳✳✳✳✳✳✳✳✳✳✳✳✳✳✳✳✳✳✳✳✳✳✳✳✳✳✳✳✳✳✳✳✳

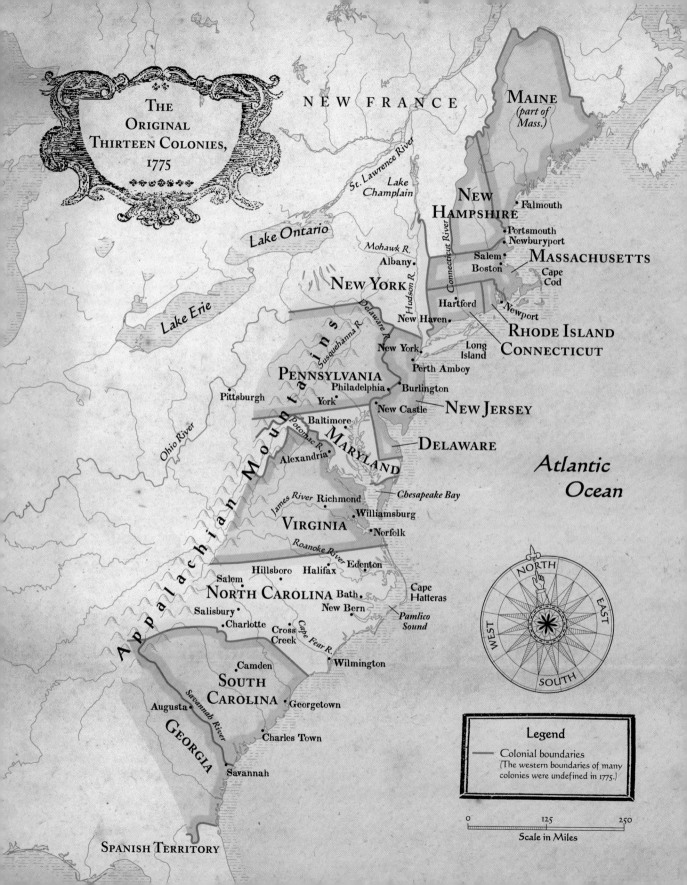

THE ORIGINAL THIRTEEN COLONIES, 1775

NEW FRANCE

MAINE
(part of Mass.)

St. Lawrence River

Lake Champlain

Lake Ontario

NEW HAMPSHIRE

• Falmouth

Mohawk R.

• Portsmouth
• Newburyport

Albany •

Salem • MASSACHUSETTS

Connecticut River

Hudson R.

Boston •

Cape Cod

Lake Erie

NEW YORK

Delaware R.

Hartford •

• Newport

New Haven •

RHODE ISLAND
CONNECTICUT

Susquehanna R.

New York •

Long Island

PENNSYLVANIA

Perth Amboy •

Philadelphia •

Burlington •

Pittsburgh •

York •

New Castle •

NEW JERSEY

Baltimore •

DELAWARE

Ohio River

Potomac R.

MARYLAND

Alexandria •

Chesapeake Bay

Atlantic Ocean

James River Richmond •

• Williamsburg

VIRGINIA

• Norfolk

Roanoke River

Hillsboro • Halifax • Edenton •

Salem •

Cape Hatteras

NORTH CAROLINA Bath •

New Bern •

Pamlico Sound

Salisbury •

• Charlotte

Cross Creek

Cape Fear R.

Camden •

• Wilmington

SOUTH CAROLINA

• Georgetown

Augusta •

Savannah River

GEORGIA

• Charles Town

Savannah •

A p p a l a c h i a n   M o u n t a i n s

SPANISH TERRITORY

NORTH
EAST
WEST
SOUTH

Legend

—— Colonial boundaries
(The western boundaries of many colonies were undefined in 1775.)

0   125   250
Scale in Miles

A Nation Grows
From Thirteen Colonies

****

Massachusetts lies in the northeastern region of the United States. It is bordered by Vermont and New Hampshire on the north, New York on the west, and Connecticut and Rhode Island on the south. Its eastern border is formed by the Atlantic Ocean.

Massachusetts was first settled in 1620 by Pilgrims who were seeking religious freedom. The local Indians greeted the Pilgrims as friends and helped them survive when they first arrived. Those same Indians would be driven out by the European newcomers.

Massachusetts grew quickly. Its largest city, Boston, would become one of the major trading centers in the American colonies. The colony would be at the center of events that led to the American Revolution.

The map shows the thirteen English colonies in 1775. The colored sections show the areas that were settled at that time.

CHAPTER ONE

Discovery

* *

The Unexpected Landing

The *Mayflower* set sail from Plymouth, England, in September 1620. The captain, Master Christopher Jones, guided the small ship and its 102 passengers through terrible storms, illnesses, and hunger. After sixty-five days at sea, those on board finally heard the words they had waited to hear: "Land ho!"

The passengers were filled with relief. They crowded onto the *Mayflower*'s deck to catch their first sight of the land.

The foul weather had blown the *Mayflower* 200 miles (320 kilometers) north of its planned destination. The ship was in the northeastern part of America known as New England. But the people on the ship were ready to bring the long, hard journey to an end. They dropped anchor and prepared themselves to start a new life.

In 1620, the Pilgrims left Europe with all of their belongings to start a new life in America.

The Pilgrims

It took a lot of courage to leave home, family, and friends to cross the wide Atlantic Ocean in the 1600s. The *Mayflower's* passengers, however, had good reasons to leave their homeland. They were Separatists. These were people who did not agree with the practices of England's official church, the Anglican Church. The Separatists wanted to find a new home where they could practice religion according to their beliefs.

The Separatists gained permission from England's King James I to create a new colony in the northern part of the English territory of Virginia. The English claimed land from present-day New York all the way to Florida. They called this huge area Virginia.

Whole families boarded a ship bound for America with the intention of staying there and making a brand-new life. They soon came to be known as Pilgrims. Pilgrims are people who journey to foreign lands.

Arrival in New England

Once in America, the Pilgrims created an agreement they called the Mayflower Compact. This document stated that they would "enact, constitute, and frame such just and equal Laws...as shall be thought...for the general good."

When the Pilgrims came ashore at Plymouth, Massachusetts, on December 22, 1620, they were faced with a cold New England winter.

In other words, they agreed to make fair laws for their settlement and live by them. Then they elected one of their number, John Carver, to be the first governor of their colony.

Next, the Pilgrims set out to find a place to settle that was protected from the weather and the sea. They had no shelter and little food, and winter would soon arrive. A small party of men set out to explore the area.

They soon discovered plenty of freshwater streams inland. More surprisingly, they found mysterious mounds of earth. When the Pilgrims dug into the mounds, they uncovered baskets of corn and beans. They had heard from past European visitors that Native Americans lived in the area. The Pilgrims decided that the food must belong to the Indians. They did not want to anger the Indians, but they

The Pilgrims lived on their ship, the Mayflower, *during their first winter in Massachusetts. The ship was anchored in Cape Cod Bay.*

were hungry so they took some of the food. They planned on paying it back when they had raised their own crops. In the meantime, they knew that without the food, their families would soon starve.

Finally, in the midst of an early snowstorm, the men found an abandoned Indian village on the shore of Cape Cod Bay. The ground had been cleared, fields were dug, and some structures had been left in place. A freshwater stream ran nearby. It looked like a good place to settle. The men hurried back to the *Mayflower* to tell the other passengers the good news. The Pilgrims named their settlement Plymouth Plantation.

The rest of the Pilgrims had been waiting in the *Mayflower*. They must have viewed the wild landscape with both hope and fear. Surely they could live free here. Yet they had heard negative reports about Native Americans. One of the Pilgrim leaders, William Bradford, had written that the natives were "savages" who "delight to torment men in the most bloody manner." Little did the Pilgrims know that it would be those same Native Americans who would save their lives.

"People of the First Light"

The explorer Giovanni da Verrazano saw the Native Americans of New England in 1524, when he traveled there. He later described them as "the goodliest people" who "exceed us in bigness, they are the color of brass...with long black hair which they carefully turn and deck up: they are of a sweet and pleasant countenance."

The Wampanoag

The area where the Pilgrims settled had been inhabited by native people for thousands of years. By 1620, nearly 5,000 Wampanoag Indians lived in what would become eastern Massachusetts. Their tribe's name meant "land where the sun comes up first." For that reason, they were known as "the people of the first light." The Wampanoag were one of numerous tribes who spoke some version, or dialect, of the Algonquian language.

The Wampanoag knew about Europeans. About 600 years earlier, Viking explorers had arrived on the Massachusetts shore. Other explorers, such as John Cabot and Giovanni da Verrazano, had visited the area in the late 1400s and early 1500s. Later, fishermen from Spain, France, Portugal, Ireland, and England regularly fished in the waters to the north. They sometimes came ashore and traded with the Indians for furs. In 1614, John Smith of the Virginia Company mapped the region.

Some of the earlier Europeans had treated the Native Americans well. Fur traders offered items that had never before been seen in the New World. (Europeans considered Europe the Old World. They called North and South America the New World.) The Native Americans happily traded their furs for European cloth, glass beads, utensils, and steel weapons.

Some Europeans, however, had kidnapped natives to sell as slaves or to take home as curiosities. Even worse, Europeans had brought some diseases to America that had wiped out entire native villages. These Europeans did not respect the native way of life or the Indians' religious **rituals**. It was no wonder that the Wampanoag avoided the Pilgrims at first.

The Sacred Pipe

The Wampanoag respected the animals, plants, and rocks that surrounded them. They believed that all of nature was connected. They performed rituals that acted out their belief in the gods of nature.

Native Americans throughout North America considered the tobacco pipe as a holy object. They grew tobacco just for the sacred pipe. Smoking the sacred pipe (also called the peace pipe) was an important part of every ceremony. The tribes performed different ceremonies involving religion, hunting, war, or peace.

For example, the Indians used ceremonies to ask for protection from the weather, from enemies, or from evil spirits. The Indians also sealed agreements and treaties by smoking the pipe.

Native Americans believed that when they smoked a pipe, the smoke carried their prayers to the gods. For this reason, they only smoked the pipe on special occasions, using it to invite good and stop evil. Children learned quickly never to touch the pipe or come near it. To do so was to put their families in danger of some terrible disaster.

Wampanoag Life

The Wampanoag lived in small villages. The villages were located where the hunting was good and the Indians could plant crops of kidney beans, corn, pumpkins, and squash. For shelter, they built round, domed houses known to the English as wigwams, or loaf-shaped buildings called long-houses. Both kinds of buildings had sapling frames covered

The forests, lakes, rivers, and seashore of Massachusetts provided the Wampanoag and other Indians with everything they needed to survive.

with mats of tightly woven reeds. When the Indians needed to find a new location because food became scarce, they could remove the mats and carry them along with them. They left the sapling frames for when they next returned.

All Wampanoag tribe members, even the children, were expected to work for the good of the whole tribe. Instead of going to school, the children learned what they needed to know by working alongside their parents.

The men and boys hunted and fished to provide the village with food. They traveled in canoes they built from burned-out tree trunks or branches and birch bark. The Indians made the tools they needed out of clamshells, animal bones, and even rocks. They hunted deer, bears, and other animals that yielded a harvest of furs, as well as food. They also hunted wild turkeys, ducks, and geese. With spears, nets, and baskets they harvested shellfish, eels, and a variety of fish.

A successful hunter always shared his catch with the family of a hunter who had not had such good luck. This helped everyone to survive. The Indians ate a lot when food was plentiful. They learned to deal with empty bellies when it was scarce.

The women and girls planted and tended the crops, preserved food by smoking or drying it, and prepared animals' skins to be used as leather or furs. The skins would be turned into **breechclouts** and leggings for the men and skirts and poncho-style shirts for the women. Moccasins and fur capes were made for everyone.

The Europeans often commented that the skin of the Native Americans appeared reddish in color. The color came from a mixture of red pigments that the natives found in the earth and grease made from the fat of bears. The natives spread this mixture on their skin. It protected them from both bitter cold winds in winter and swarms of biting insects in summer.

Plymouth Plantation

The English settlers did not know how to live in the wilderness the way the Native Americans did. They had grown up in English towns and on farms. By the time they arrived in Plymouth, it was too late in the year to gather food or plant crops. The cold days and frostbitten land made building almost impossible. During their first winter in New England, the Pilgrims lived aboard the *Mayflower*.

The men who were healthy and strong enough started building Plymouth Plantation. The first structure they built was a storehouse for the supplies brought from England. The supplies included bedding, preserved food and flour, tools, hardware, and weapons for self-defense and hunting. The storehouse was also used as a place to recover from illness and to gather for worship and group meetings.

The Pilgrims built wood-framed houses with thatched roofs using the materials they found in the new colony.

The Pilgrims quickly ran short of supplies. They had sold some of their goods before they left England. They had consumed much of their food during their long sea voyage. When a spark from the fireplace set fire to the roof of the storehouse, most of their remaining supplies went up in smoke. Before the winter had ended, half the *Mayflower*'s passengers and crew had died of starvation, disease, or the cold, wet climate. The survivors spent much of the winter tending the sick and burying the dead.

Finally, spring arrived, and the Pilgrims planted their first crops. Just as important, a surprise visitor who would change their lives walked into their settlement. The man was an Algonquian chief named Samoset. Much to the Pilgrims' amazement, he greeted them with the English words he had learned from English fishermen.

Samoset told the Pilgrims about the Wampanoag who lived in the region. Within days, Samoset returned with the Wampanoag chief, called a sachem. An Indian interpreter named Squanto came with them. Squanto had once lived in

the village the Pilgrims had found. He had been kidnapped by Englishmen and taken to Europe. When he returned home, Squanto learned that his entire tribe had been wiped out by disease.

Wattle and Daub

To build their houses, the Pilgrims used a method called wattle and daub. This method required few tools or extra supplies.

First, wooden posts were set up in rows to make walls. Then the poles were connected by weaving small branches (wattle) between them. To create a kind of cement (daub), the Pilgrims mixed chopped-up marsh grass, water, and clay from the ground. This they smeared onto the woven walls to make them air- and watertight. The Pilgrims **thatched** their roofs with straw or grass.

Wattle and daub was an easy method of building that sealed the walls from wind and cold.

The Pilgrim and Native American leaders soon made a treaty of peace. They promised not to steal from each other or harm each other. They also pledged to help each other if a war with other Indians or Europeans should occur. Squanto, meanwhile, lived with the Pilgrims and taught them Indian ways to survive.

The First Thanksgiving

The Pilgrims had struggled in order to establish a settlement on New England soil. Half their number had died, including Governor Carver. The Pilgrims appointed William Bradford to replace him.

Early colonists gathered to share a meal together.

By the autumn of 1621, however, the Pilgrims had something to celebrate. One year after their arrival, the Plymouth settlers brought in a good harvest of vegetables. "Being all well recovered in health and strength," as Governor Bradford later wrote, "they had all things in good plenty."

The Pilgrims invited Massasoit, the Wampanoag sachem, to join them in a celebration of thanksgiving to God. Massasoit arrived with ninety of his people and five freshly killed deer for the feast. The English and the Native Americans stayed together for three days, feasting, playing, and performing military drills. This feast developed into the modern holiday of Thanksgiving.

The Pilgrims would suffer more times of scarce food and disease. Unfriendly tribes would challenge them. New arrivals from England would come and demand land. But the Pilgrims had formed England's first lasting settlement in New England. This was the first step toward the formation of the colony of Massachusetts.

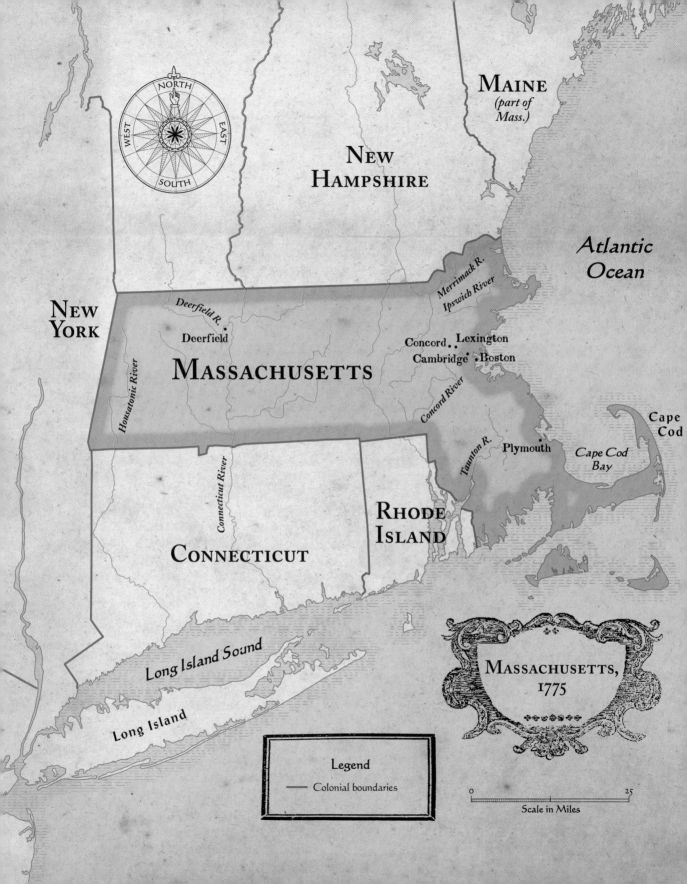

NORTH
EAST
WEST
SOUTH

MAINE
(part of Mass.)

NEW
HAMPSHIRE

Atlantic
Ocean

NEW
YORK

Merrimack R.
Ipswich River

Deerfield R.

Deerfield

Concord • Lexington
Cambridge • Boston

MASSACHUSETTS

Housatonic River

Concord River

Cape
Cod

Taunton R.
Plymouth

Cape Cod
Bay

Connecticut River

RHODE
ISLAND

CONNECTICUT

Long Island Sound

MASSACHUSETTS,
1775

Long Island

Legend
— Colonial boundaries

0   25
Scale in Miles

CHAPTER TWO

The Massachusetts Bay Colony

****

A New Colony

The Plymouth colony grew slowly. In the small settlement at Plymouth Plantation, the colonists continued to live close together. They helped each other clear land for crops, hunt and gather food, and build shelters for their families. The need for protection was never far from their minds.

The Wampanoag remained friends with the Pilgrims, but other tribes were angry that the English had moved into their traditional hunting grounds. The Pilgrims had to be ready to defend themselves at all times. In 1627, a visitor to Plymouth from England wrote, "They are constantly on their guard night and day." Men went to church, he reported, carrying their muskets. During the service, "each sets his arms [gun] down near him."

This map shows how Massachusetts looked in 1775.

The Great Migration

While Plymouth settlers were learning to survive in America, another group of people in England were making plans to go to New England. These people were known as Puritans. The Puritans, like the Separatists, disagreed with the teachings of the Anglican Church. They wanted to find a new place to live where they could practice their form of religion freely—worshipping, studying the Bible, and governing themselves according to what they believed the Bible taught.

In March 1629, John Winthrop and a group of Puritans in England formed the Massachusetts Bay Company. They secured a **charter** from England's king, Charles I, for a new colony. The charter gave them permission to claim land in America north of Plymouth and name it the Massachusetts Bay Colony. They were also given the right to form a colonial government to rule themselves in the New World.

With the settlement of these two colonies, people from England began to pour into New England. The flow of newcomers, called the Great Migration, lasted from 1630 to 1640. It included more than 300 ships carrying about 21,000 men, women, and children. Most of them were Puritans.

John Winthrop led the first large group of colonists to the Massachusetts Bay Colony in 1630. His fleet of eleven

In 1630, John Winthrop's fleet of eleven ships sailed into Boston Harbor with a large group of settlers, farm animals, and supplies.

ships carried 1,000 passengers, as well as hundreds of cows, horses, pigs, goats, and chickens. On board the ship *Arbella*, Winthrop delivered a **sermon** that would later become famous. He instructed the colonists to keep their covenant, or agreement, with God and each other. Their community, he declared, would be like a "city on a hill." All the world would watch the people in the settlement and learn from them. Before the year ended, another six ships arrived with 500 more settlers.

Massachusetts Bay colonists arrived as families. They were ready to stay in America and make it their new home. They paid their way by selling their property in England. Many of them brought their servants and furnishings with them. In the ships, they stowed farm animals and large quantities of food, nails, glass, iron, guns, and ammunition that would help them start their new life.

"A City on a Hill"

Winthrop was elected the first governor of Massachusetts Bay Colony. He remained in that position for seventeen years. He helped choose a place for the capital of the colony, which the settlers named Boston. During his first year, he also helped pass a law allowing all free male citizens who were members of the Puritan church to vote. Every year, these "freemen" elected a governor, a **deputy** governor, assistants, and deputies. This group of leaders was called the General Court.

The first Massachusetts Bay settlers did not have an easy time. One man related that when he first arrived in Boston, "for lack of housing [I had] to find shelter at night in an empty cask [a barrel used for liquids]." Another newcomer reported that the settlers in a nearby area had built "some [English] wigwams and one house" by the time he arrived. Many others, however, lived in flimsy tents.

"The poorer sort of people," John Winthrop wrote, "were much afflicted with scurvy [a disease caused by a lack of fresh vegetables and fruits in the diet] and many died." Another settler reported, "Yet, they sang psalms, praised, and prayed to their God till they could provide themselves homes."

Most Pilgrim leaders were also ministers. They delivered both political and religious messages during church services.

Each settler received 50 acres (20 hectares) for free. People who bought a share in the Massachusetts Bay Company were entitled to 200 acres (80 hectares) of land. If they paid to transport a servant, they received 50 acres (20 hectares) more. So many colonists were now hurrying from England to the colony that settlements soon spread into the countryside surrounding Boston. Before long, the colonists had created many villages with churches, taverns, houses, craftsmen's shops, mills, and farms.

Village Life

Puritans believed that people needed to go to church every Sunday and live a religious life day to day. So the General Court said that each town must have its own church, called a meetinghouse. The Puritans gathered at the meetinghouse for both religious worship and town meetings. Houses were built along a single street next to the meetinghouse. An area of grassy public land called a **green** was placed right in the middle of the town. Often, livestock would graze on the green. The men of the town would gather there to train as a local **militia**, a military group of citizen soldiers.

The open land outside the town and beyond the houses was divided into fields for farming. In addition, each household had a kitchen garden for vegetables and herbs and a small orchard for fruit trees. Single people were not

The Puritans and Holidays

The Puritans did not celebrate any Christian holidays because the Bible did not say they should. They celebrated Days of Thanksgiving. They often spent the whole day fasting (not eating) and praying. They also celebrated the Sabbath, beginning on every Saturday night and ending at sundown on Sunday evening.

Only churchgoing, family prayer, thinking about God, and Bible reading were allowed on the Sabbath. No one was allowed to cook, clean, make beds, travel, play, or do any "unnecessary and unseasonable walking in the streets and fields." A man who kissed his wife in public on the Sabbath might be punished for "lewd and unseemly behavior."

allowed to live alone or in pairs. Households often included both family members and young unmarried men or women.

The Puritans considered education extremely important. After all, a person had to know how to read in order to study the Bible. In 1635, America's first secondary school (high school), called the Boston Latin School, was founded. A year later, Harvard College, the first college in the colonies, began classes to train young men as ministers. In 1638, Massachusetts created its first library in Boston. A year after that, a printer named Stephen Daye set up the first printing press in America in the Massachusetts town of Cambridge. The press made more books available,

The Puritan Watchdog

Winthrop's "city on a hill" depended on people living "holy" lives. So the General Court appointed tithing men.

A tithing man had charge over a group of ten families. He made sure that everyone under his watch attended church unless they were ill. He also inspected taverns and reported unruly conduct. He forced "undesirable" people (people who did not obey the law) out of town. During church services, he shooed away stray dogs and hit the knuckles of rowdy children with a "church stick." The stick had a rabbit's foot on one end and a foxtail on the other. He would use the foxtail to tickle awake anyone who snoozed before the hours-long sermon ended.

making it easier for people to study. By 1640, there were 300 college-trained Puritan ministers serving in churches throughout the colony. In 1647, the General Court ordered that any town with fifty or more families must have its own elementary school.

People in the Massachusetts Bay Colony also had rules about how to dress. In 1651, the General Court ordered that those who wore clothing that was too fancy for their jobs or rank in society would have to pay a fine. Anyone not worth at least 200 pounds (British money equal to about $32,000 today) in personal wealth, for example, could "not wear any gold or silver lace, or gold and silver buttons, or silk hoods, or scarfs."

No Differences Allowed

The members of the General Court made it their business to keep the settlers focused on God. The court passed laws against what it considered activities that distracted people from thinking about God. Attending plays, dancing around a Maypole, bowling on the green, and playing

The Pilgrims built the first church in New England, where they met for religious services every week.

shuffleboard, quoits (horseshoes), dice, or cards were all forbidden.

The leaders of the Massachusetts Bay Colony watched for people whose religious ideas were different from the Puritans' own. One such man was Roger Williams, the minister in the town of Salem. Williams had come to the colony with John Winthrop's fleet in 1630. Within five years, Williams decided that he disagreed with Winthrop's ideas. Williams believed that religion and government should be kept separate. Winthrop believed that the colony would succeed as a "city on a hill" only if the government was based on religious ideas.

The General Court voted to banish Williams from the colony for his different ideas. This meant he had to leave and never come back. He fled south to what would become Rhode Island. He was joined two years later by Anne Hutchinson. Hutchinson had gotten in trouble with the General Court for claiming that God spoke directly to her. (The Puritans believed that God spoke only through the words of the Bible.)

Handmade in America

The lives of ordinary people in the Massachusetts Bay Colony were filled with the business of home, farm, and skilled work. It cost a lot of money to **import** items such as

Roger Williams was taken in by the Narragansett Indians in Rhode Island after he was thrown out of Massachusetts Bay Colony.

clothes and furnishings from England. So the colonists made by hand much of what they needed themselves.

People raised sheep for wool. Most households had a spinning wheel and loom. The wool was shaved from the sheep's hides every spring. The women and children would then use the spinning wheel to spin the wool into yarn.

Every colonial household needed soap for washing clothes. At first, people imported soap from England by the firkin (a barrel holding nine gallons). Soon, however, colonial women started making their own soap once or twice a year.

One essential soap ingredient, tallow, came from the fat of animals that the colonists butchered for food. The fat had to be rendered. This process of boiling the fat with water removed impurities so the fat would not smell bad.

The other essential ingredient of soap was lye, which came from ash. The colonists had plenty of ash left over from burning wood for cooking and keeping warm. The ash was loaded into a bottomless barrel that had been placed atop a stone with a groove carved into it. The soap maker then poured water over the ash. This produced a brownish liquid known as potash lye. The lye flowed along the stone's groove and into a clay pot placed under its edge.

The soap maker then mixed the lye and tallow together in a large pot and boiled the mixture over a fire for six to eight hours. After it had formed a thick, frothy mass, she would taste it. When it did not burn the tongue, it was ready to be used as soft soap.

They then stretched the yarn over the frame of the loom and wove it into fabric for clothes and blankets. To add color to their cloth, New Englanders made dyes by boiling berries, flowers like irises and goldenrod, and bark from red oak and hickory trees. The dyes could be used to color either the yarn or the finished cloth.

Electric lights did not exist, so most work was done during the daytime. Most people rose when the sun came up and went to bed at dark. They also came up with sources of artificial light so they could continue to work and read the Bible in the evening hours. Francis Higginson, one of the colony's early ministers, explained that

> *the abundance of the fish [in New England]*
> *can afford oil for lamps. Yea, our pine trees,*
> *that are the most plentiful of all wood, doth allow*
> *us plenty of candles which are very useful in the*
> *house; and they are such candles as the Indians*
> *commonly use...nothing else but the wood of the*
> *pine tree cloven [split] into little slices something*
> *thin, which are so full of the moisture of turpentine*
> *and pitch, that they burn as clear as a torch.*

When cattle became more plentiful, people used tallow to make candles. Tallow came from the animals' fat. A person making candles dipped strings into hot tallow. Between dips, the tallow was allowed to dry. After many dips, the layers of dried tallow made the candle thick enough to use. Later, in the 1700s, whaling would provide whale oil to burn in lamps.

Changing Times

Migration to the Massachusetts Bay Colony slowed around 1640. However, the colony kept growing as the children of the first settlers became adults who needed land of their own. The English continued to spread through the region, claiming more and more of the Native Americans' land. One tribe in southern New England, called the Pequot, decided that the colonists had moved onto enough of the land that the Pequot considered theirs.

The Indians who killed John Oldham lived on Block Island. They were attacked by colonial militia during the Pequot War.

Settlers and Pequot fought small battles over land and trading rights for several years. Then a man named John Oldham was killed by a neighboring tribe. The Pequot hid the Indians who had killed Oldham, refusing to turn them over to the Connecticut militia. The militia asked for help from Massachusetts.

In 1637, the Massachusetts Bay Colony sent armed men to help the English settlers in the Connecticut region fight against the Pequot. On May 26, the English forced their way into a Pequot fort and set fire to the wigwams inside. As the Indians escaped from their burning homes, the English shot them. Within half an hour, more than 600 Indian men, women, and children died. Over the next two months, the English killed many of the Pequot who escaped. They sold the rest as slaves to other tribes. The once-powerful Pequot tribe was reduced to only a few remaining families.

John Winthrop died in 1649, leaving his "city on a hill" to younger leaders. Eight years later, in 1657, Plymouth's leader, William Bradford, died. A new generation of leaders, many of them born in the New World, would now be in charge.

CHAPTER THREE

Trial by Fire for a Growing Colony

****

Struggles for Control

By the mid-1600s, Massachusetts Bay was becoming a bustling, prospering colony. People pushed farther inland to find areas to settle. In seeking new homes, they claimed more and more land that Native Americans considered their own.

Many Indian tribes feared that they would lose their lands altogether unless they put up a fight against the colonists. Others remembered what had happened to the Pequot and did not want to suffer the same fate. But one Indian leader tried to unite the tribes in order to drive the European settlers from their lands.

Wampanoag chief Metacomet led a rebellion against the English colonists who were taking more and more Indian lands.

Chief Massasoit, the colonists' friend, had died. His son, Metacomet, called King Philip by the colonists, now led the Wampanoag people. Metacomet did not share his father's friendliness toward the English. Instead, he spoke out strongly against them. He encouraged all the region's tribes to stand up and fight for their land.

King Philip's War

In 1675, the English colonists charged three Wampanoag with committing a crime against an Indian who had converted to Christianity. The Indians were put on trial in the colonial court, found guilty, and executed.

The surrounding tribes did not believe that the English had the right to put a Native American on trial. When news of the executions spread, one tribe after another joined the Wampanoag in furious attacks against colonial villages. The natives burned houses and destroyed cattle and crops. They killed men, women, and children.

Terrified, colonial militias from all over Massachusetts loaded their muskets and marched off to war against King Philip's followers. In the following months, no one could tell which side was winning. As the war grew fiercer, it spread to other parts of New England.

In the end, the Native Americans were doomed. There were twice as many English colonists in the region as Indians.

The Indian leader, Metacomet, was killed in August 1676, ending King Philip's War.

By 1676, when the war was over, 600 English settlers had died. Fifty-two out of ninety colonial towns were destroyed, including 1,200 homes and 8,000 cattle. Many other towns were badly damaged. Meanwhile, the Native Americans lost 3,000 lives. Hundreds more Indians were shipped to other countries as slaves. The native people of southern New England had lost their land once and for all.

The New England Family

It would take years for the people of the Massachusetts Bay Colony to recover from the cost and horror of King Philip's War. Yet life went on, and the colony continued to grow.

The colonists had big families, often having at least six or seven children. People carefully recorded every birth, name, baptism, and death. Such records were kept in the blank pages of family Bibles. These records show that many families had more than a dozen children.

Many children were named after people from the Bible, such as Abigail, Rachel, Joshua, and Joseph. Other children's names reflected their parents' feelings and hopes. Such names as Comfort, Deliverance, Silence, and Patience fill the pages of colonial family Bibles.

Homes in colonial Massachusetts must have been noisy, busy places with so many children there. The older children took care of the younger ones. They helped keep the fires burning for warmth and cooking. They carried buckets full of water from wells or nearby streams for the household.

The girls helped at the hearth, or fireplace, cooking the day's beef and peas or bean porridge. They also baked bread for the coming week. They fed the chickens and pigs, milked the cows, and churned butter.

One of the most important jobs on every colonial farm was to milk the cow every day. This chore was often done by young boys or girls.

The boys led the cattle and sheep to pasture in the morning and locked them in their pens at night. They helped to clear land of trees and rocks, plow the ground, sow the year's crops, and cut the hay. If a boy's father was a craftsman, such as a cooper (barrel maker) or blacksmith, the boy worked with his father in the shop.

Things quieted down at mealtime. Children were not supposed to speak unless asked a question. They stood at the table to eat while the adults sat. Mealtime usually included a time of family prayer, Bible reading, and teaching. After dinner, the family often gathered around the hearth for light and warmth. The girls would practice their sewing on small, stitched pictures called samplers. The boys would practice carving wood or help mend fishing nets, tools, or furniture.

Hornbooks and Primers

In Massachusetts, the General Court made sure that all children went to school. If a family lived too far away from a school for children to attend, the children were sent to stay with relatives who lived near a school. Sometimes, ministers invited country boys to live with the ministers' families in order to receive schooling. Reading was the most important skill to learn. The Puritans wanted their children to be able to read the Bible so they would know more about God and

Paying for School

In colonial Massachusetts, students had to pay for school. Because money was scarce, students often paid their teachers with Indian corn, wheat, peas, or beans. If their father traded in furs, students might show up with beaver pelts. They even offered wampum, which was the Native American form of money. Wampum was usually in the form of a belt that had been woven with a design of beads made out of shells.

Like every building in the colony, the one-room schoolhouses were cold in winter. The teacher expected students' parents to provide the logs for the schoolhouse fireplace. If a family did not contribute its fair share of firewood, that family's children were likely to be seated in the coldest corner of the room.

A wood-burning stove provided the only heat for many one-room schoolhouses.

about how to live. Writing and arithmetic were good to know, but they did not make a person a better Christian.

Paper was hard to get in colonial New England, so a child's first schoolbook came in the form of a hornbook instead of a book with many pages. A hornbook was a piece

Colonial children learned to read using a hornbook.

of wood in the shape of a paddle. On the wood was tacked a single sheet of paper with a thin, transparent piece of animal horn over it. The horn protected the paper from tearing or getting wet so it would last a long time. The alphabet was printed across the top of the page. This was followed by simple syllables such as "ab," "eb," "ib," and "ob." Following this was the Lord's Prayer.

The next book used to teach reading was called a primer. *The New England Primer* became the most famous primer ever published. Aside from the alphabet and syllables, it included morning, mealtime, and evening prayers. It offered a catechism, which was a series of questions and answers about the Bible. It became especially well known for the rhymes it used to teach the alphabet, from "In Adam's fall, / We sinned all" to "Zaccheus he, / Did climb a tree, / His Lord to see."

Students often practiced writing or did their "sums" (arithmetic) on pieces of birch bark. They used pens made from goose quills and ink that was a mixture of ink powder and water. It was an important part of a child's education to learn how to use a pen without splattering ink.

"Spare the Rod, Spoil the Child"

The colonists were firm believers in the "rod" as an aid to teaching. If a student did not pay attention, talked out of turn, or disobeyed a rule, punishment would always follow.

Sometimes, students were punished by being spanked. Other times, students' knuckles were rapped with an actual rod made of a birch branch. The teacher might give a student a "thimmel-pie," which was a sharp thump on the head with a **thimble**. A child who did too much talking might have to wear a "whispering stick." This was a piece of wood placed in the mouth like a gag and tied in place with string.

Parents and teachers did not think they were being mean when they punished the children. They believed that it was their duty to teach the children how to be good Christian citizens. The Bible said, "Spare the rod, spoil the child." The Puritans thought this meant that without punishment ("the rod"), children would naturally misbehave.

England Takes Control

While Massachusetts was trying to return to normal life after King Philip's War, England was taking a new look at the colonies. England's power and **prosperity** depended on world trade. English craftsmen produced a wide variety of manufactured goods, such as cloth, clothing, hardware, tools, furniture, dishes, glass, and silverware. The English traded these for goods they needed from around the world.

The American colonies were one of England's sources for such goods. The colonies produced rice, indigo (a plant that could be made into blue dye), wheat, rum, lumber, and tobacco. As Massachusetts grew, its merchants offered a good trade in fish, furs, and materials for building ships. England wanted all of these items.

By the late 1600s, England knew it had to make some changes if it was going to remain the strongest, richest country in the world. King Charles II and his government (Parliament) decided that England needed to make much more profit from the trade coming out of the colonies.

In 1676, Parliament sent Edmund Randolph to Massachusetts to see how the colony was run. Right away, Randolph started complaining that the people of the colony disobeyed trade laws. He said this was costing England huge sums of money. He also accused the colonists of mistreating people who were not Puritans, especially members of the Anglican Church.

When King Charles II died in 1685 his brother James became king. King James II took action. He canceled the Massachusetts Bay Colony's charter. Then he combined New Hampshire, Massachusetts, Plymouth, Rhode Island, and Connecticut to form the Dominion of New England. He got rid of the Massachusetts General Court and the colony's elected governor. The king made Sir Edmund Andros from the colony of New York the royal governor of Massachusetts.

Andros, like Randolph, was disliked by the people of Massachusetts. He replaced local leaders with people appointed by the king. He limited the number of town meetings and local elections the colonists could hold. He took over free land that colonists used for timber or pasture. He even tried to raise taxes. When merchants protested, he had them arrested and fined.

Sir Edmund Andros was the governor of the Dominion of New England from 1685 until 1689.

Andros also made a law that required people to pay for land they already owned. Even worse, he withdrew the public money that was used to support the Puritan churches. Then he built the colony's first non-Puritan church, which was Anglican.

Early on April 18, 1689, angry crowds of colonists gathered in Boston. By noon, Puritan leaders, merchants, and militiamen took charge. They arrested Andros and

Randolph. Then they forced British troops, which had been stationed in Boston and the harbor, to surrender. The colony returned to operating in the way it had under the old charter.

The Witch Scare

By the end of the 1600s, the people of the Massachusetts Bay Colony had been through many troubles. King Philip's war had made the colony poorer. The British takeover of their government had left the colonists worried and angry. To the Puritans, such troubles seemed to show that God was punishing them. One famous Puritan minister proclaimed that the devil had tempted them to care more about worldly things than they did about God. These beliefs may have made it easier for people to explain a series of strange and frightening events.

In 1692, the daughter of the Salem minister, Reverend Samuel Parris, and a group of her friends claimed that witches were attacking them. The witches, they said, were women in their own village of Salem. Many people, including the Puritans, had long believed that witches were servants of the devil.

When the governor of the colony, Sir William Phips, heard the girls' accusations, he took them seriously. He set up a special court to bring the suspected witches to trial.

In 1692, people accused of witchcraft were put on trial in Salem.
A guilty verdict meant severe punishment, including being put to death.

During the trials, the girls accused many more people of being witches. As the trials continued, more of Salem's citizens came forward with wild stories of witchcraft.

The court met through the spring and summer of 1692. Before the witch scare ended, twenty people had been **condemned** as witches and executed. Hundreds more were accused, and about 150 were put in prison. Some of these people died before they could be tried. Others remained behind bars awaiting their fate. The accusers even put two dogs to death because they were thought to be helping the Devil.

Soon, people from nearby towns began to realize that the people accused of witchcraft were being blamed for things they had not done. The General Court in Boston insisted that the trials be stopped. Eventually, those who remained in prison were declared innocent and set free.

Changes Ahead

Parliament granted a new charter to the people of Massachusetts in 1692. The new charter required that Puritan leaders accept the different religious views of others. The leaders knew that change would come about as the population grew and the farms and businesses multiplied. They hoped that the changes would bring better times. They were tired of war and trouble. They did not know that their biggest battles were still ahead of them.

CHAPTER FOUR

The Colony Thrives

****

A Growing Colony

By the early 1700s, the colonists of Massachusetts Bay had turned the rocky wilderness of New England into a busy, prospering region. In 1700, about 6,700 people lived in Boston. By 1740, that number had grown to 16,000. Much of that growth came from people who were born in the colony. Families were large, and the good food and healthy conditions of New England meant that many children survived to be adults. These healthy conditions made the population larger in another way. People who grew up in New England were on average more than three inches taller than people who grew up in Europe.

Many new immigrants arrived in the colony as well. Most of them came from England, though people came from other European countries, too. Some of the newcomers who could not afford to pay for the trip chose to

By the early 1700s, Boston was a well-established, busy city, the center of a growing colony.

51

become indentured servants. This meant that someone paid their way. Indentured servants then paid the money back by working for that person for five to seven years. When their time was up, indentured servants were free. They could open businesses and own land. Some masters gave their former servants tools or money to help them get started in their new lives.

Slaves in New England

Some people came to Massachusetts against their will. These were slaves, usually Africans who had been enslaved to work on the sugar plantations of the West Indies. The people of Boston bought slaves during periods when fewer workers from Europe were arriving. Such periods occurred, for example, when war in Europe made travel to America difficult. Then slaves would be imported so there were enough workers for the colony's businesses.

Even though the people of Massachusetts did not own many slaves themselves, the merchants of Massachusetts did a great deal of trade in the slave market. They helped pay for the "stealing" (capturing) of people in Africa. These people were then sent to the West Indies and the southern American colonies to work on plantations. The New England merchants made good profits on the capturing, buying, and selling of enslaved people.

Slaves were brought to Massachusetts from Africa and the Caribbean islands to work in America.

Merchants and magistrates (people in government) put slaves to work in the shipbuilding industry, on the wharves, and in the craftsmen's shops. Bostonians with some wealth often had a few slaves working in their homes as well.

Not everyone believed that slavery should be allowed. Some Puritans objected for religious reasons. Samuel Sewall, the judge in the Salem witch trials, wrote a tract (religious pamphlet) on the subject in 1700. The tract was called *The Selling of Joseph*. "It is most certain," Sewall wrote, "that all men…have the right unto liberty, and all other comforts of life." Other colonists, however, thought that slavery was no worse than indenture. Of all the American colonists, the people of New England kept the fewest slaves.

Trouble on the Frontier

As the coastal towns and cities grew, people pushed farther inland to make new towns. They established frontier towns like Deerfield in western Massachusetts. There was more land available to farm on the frontier, but the towns were a long way from help in case of attack.

The threat of Indian attacks was a real problem for frontier settlers. In addition, the frontier towns were in territory claimed by France. Both France and England claimed the territory of western Massachusetts. The French and the Indians banded together to prevent English settlers from taking more land.

In the summer of 1703, the 260 settlers in Deerfield received terrifying news. French and Indian soldiers were marching toward Deerfield. The settlers left their homes and moved into a fort they had built. The fort was surrounded by high walls so the settlers felt they were safe inside. They waited for an attack, but it did not come. In October, two men were captured by Indians outside the fort, but there was still no attack.

*In the early 1700s, settlers on the Massachusetts frontier were
constantly on the alert for attacks from Indians and French soldiers.*

The settlers remained in their fort as winter arrived. They waited and watched for months as the temperature fell and snow covered the ground. Finally, on the snow-covered morning of February 29, 1704, just before dawn, more than 200 French and Indian troops sneaked up on the town. The snow hid the sound of their approach. The snowdrifts against the fort's walls made it easy for the attackers to climb over the walls.

The French and Indian attack on Deerfield burned the village to the ground.

The Indians and French attacked the surprised villagers and burned their houses to the ground. Fifty-six Deerfield men, women, and children were killed. Another 109 were captured and forced to march back to the French colony of New France (Canada) with the French troops.

The French and Indians did not attack other Massachusetts towns. The settlers in western Massachusetts lived in peace for years, but they never forgot the attack on Deerfield. When the people of Massachusetts were called to fight against the French and their Indian **allies** years later, they would eagerly join the fight.

The Merchants

Meanwhile, the coastal cities and towns continued to grow. Massachusetts Bay's success depended heavily on its merchants. These were men whose business was trade between New England, the West Indies, and Europe. They created ways for the colonists to sell what they made to others and, in turn, buy what they wanted or needed.

Merchants brought goods to the colony that the colonists could not produce themselves. From the West Indies, they imported sugar, molasses, and slaves. From England, they brought tea, fine furniture, dishware, and the fancy fabrics of London.

Building a Ship

It took a lot of workers to make a ship. Shipyards hired all the different artisans (craftsmen) needed. The shipwright was the expert shipbuilder. Carpenters and joiners (workers who joined separate pieces of wood) did much of the actual building.

Smiths created all the iron hardware needed. Caulkers made the seams in the ship's construction waterproof by filling them with rope and pine pitch (a thick, sticky liquid from under a tree's bark). Rope and sail makers made the ship's rigging.

Massachusetts became well known as a source of fish, especially codfish and sturgeon. The colony's large fishing boats would bring great catches of fish into the wharves of Boston, Salem, and other port towns. The fish were then dried or salted. Merchants would sell them to the West Indies and Europe.

Massachusetts's **abundance** of woodlands also allowed the colony to produce lumber and build ships. Lumber companies sold huge tree trunks to England to be used as masts on ships built there. But England did not have enough forestland to supply wood to build many ships itself. So ships built in the colony became another item that the merchants of Massachusetts could sell across the Atlantic. Investors paid for the work and supplies. When the ship was put into use or sold, the investors were paid back and earned a **profit**.

Records were kept of every ship that arrived in Boston harbor or sailed out of the city. The records show that many different kinds of goods were sent on their way from the city's docks. Not all of those goods came from Massachusetts. Boston had become the most important port for shipping goods from all of the colonies. Cargoes included salt, rum, tobacco, pork, whale oil, cranberries, corn, candles, and cotton. Ships coming in delivered such luxuries as combs, scissors, carpenter's tools, rugs, lace, needles, pins, buttons, and candlesticks.

Boston's Craftsmen

The city of Boston buzzed with activity. In Boston's taverns and coffeehouses, merchants gathered to talk and make deals. When they were done, they would stroll out into the city. There, artisans' shops lined either side of the narrow, winding streets. Inside the shops, people made casks and barrels, hats of beaver fur, silver and gold buckles, fine suits of clothing, and iron tools and hardware.

With so much business going on and so many people living in a small area, Boston needed plenty of artisans. People who lived in the country and ran farms made many of the things they needed themselves. City dwellers did not. They depended on the craftsmen to supply what they did not buy from the merchants.

The School of Hard Work

Parents paid for their sons to become apprentices to master craftsmen. A master might be a shipwright, cordwainer (shoe-maker), carpenter, baker, miller, or some other kind of tradesman. The apprentice lived with the master's family. The master gave him clothes, food, and sometimes even lessons in reading and writing.

An apprenticeship usually lasted seven years or until the boy turned twenty-one. During that time, the apprentice could not borrow money or get married without the permission of his master. He was not allowed to find another master or start a shop of his own. If he did not show promise in a certain craft, he might be sent home to his parents. They would then try him in another trade. This was true of a young Boston lad named Benjamin Franklin.

Franklin started with a candle maker and then went on to a cutler (a maker of knives and other cutting tools). Finally, he was apprenticed to a printer. At last, he had found a job that fit him. While he was an apprentice, however, he did what many apprentices did. He ran away. Franklin settled in Philadelphia, Pennsylvania. He would later become one of colo-nial America's most famous

Like a farmer's sons working the fields, a craftsman's sons were likely to work at his trade with him. If the father had too many sons for the amount of work he did, he might send one or more off to be apprenticed to another artisan. Boston boys often became apprentices in their early teens. People called them "leather apron boys" because they wore leather aprons and breeches. Leather made good work clothes, because it did not wear out as quickly as wool or linen.

Water Power

Some work took a long time to do by hand. In the early days of settlement, the colonists of Massachusetts built mills along rivers, streams, and waterfalls. A mill allowed certain kinds of work to be done by a machine. The mill had a large paddlewheel that was partly **submerged** in the water. The flowing water pushed the submerged paddles and turned the wheel. The wheel, in turn, was attached to a rod that made a machine run.

In the Massachusetts Bay Colony, people even used the water along the coast to power mills. They would dig special ponds to capture the water when the tide came in to shore. When the tide went back out, the water in the pond emptied along a channel that contained the mill's paddlewheel.

One type of mill, called a sawmill, turned logs into finished lumber. Before this mill was invented, logs had to be sawed into boards by hand. One man stood in a deep pit while another stood on the ground above. The log to be cut would be placed like a bridge over the pit. The two men would then operate a long saw that had a handle at each end. With a sawmill, many more logs could be cut in the same amount of time it would take two men to cut one log by hand.

Gristmills were used to grind grain between two huge stone disks. The lower stone did not move. The waterwheel turned the upper stone, which ground the grain into flour.

As English as the English

As businesses grew, the people of Massachusetts became wealthier. The children and the grandchildren of the Puritan founders did not share the strict views of their elders. They saw nothing wrong in using their new wealth to buy luxuries that came to the colony on merchant ships.

Women of colonial Massachusetts began dressing more like these English women instead of wearing traditional Puritan clothes, which were much plainer and less colorful.

The Great Awakening

By the 1730s, Puritan ministers often complained that people cared more for fancy possessions than for God. But in 1734 and 1735, the minister Jonathan Edwards preached a series of sermons that got people excited about religion. This was the beginning of what was later called "the Great Awakening."

Four years later, an English preacher named George Whitefield arrived in America. Whitefield spread the religious excitement to many more people. He traveled from city to city. Everywhere he went, he caused a great **hubbub** among the people who heard him preach. Benjamin Franklin wrote that "one could not walk through town...without hearing psalms sung [on] every street." When Whitefield preached in Boston, 23,000 people came to hear him. That was more than the number of people who lived in the city.

Many of the people of Massachusetts had never lived in England, but they still considered themselves English. In the first half of the 1700s, they felt loyal to the country and wanted to live the way people did there.

People began to wear clothes that looked like the clothes worn in London, England's capital city. Men wore lace at their collars and wrists. They bought waistcoats (vests) made from rich brocades (fabrics with fancy woven designs). Women wore silk and a shiny fabric called taffeta. Under their long skirts, they wore hoops that made the skirts balloon out. Many people wore wigs or powdered their hair. Everyone wore stockings and shoes with buckles.

Massachusetts homes became more like those in England. People put aside the rough, plain furniture of the early days, especially in the cities. In its place they bought fancy furniture, rugs, draperies, and china dishes. They served English tea from silver trays. Tea had been too expensive for the colonists in the 1600s. In the middle of the 1700s, it became a favorite drink in both the cities and the country towns. Some country folk were sometimes confused about how to use the tea leaves. They put the leaves in hot water and then threw out the liquid and ate the leaves.

More Trouble

The Massachusetts colony's loyalty to England was put to the test in 1740, when England and France went to war. The war once again caused fighting on American soil. In 1745, the Massachusetts militia joined the fight. Massachusetts governor William Shirley sent 4,000 men and boys to march to Louisbourg in New France. There, he instructed the soldiers to take control of a French fort that guarded the St. Lawrence River. This river was a major route into North America.

Massachusetts lost 150 soldiers in the fight. However, the colonial troops were successful. The survivors took over the fort. Before they could complete their duty there, half of them died of a disease called dysentery. When England

The French fort at Louisbourg on the St. Lawrence River in present-day Nova Scotia, Canada, is still standing today.

made a treaty with France to stop the fighting in 1748, England returned Louisbourg to the French. The people of Massachusetts began to wonder whether the English government cared about all that the colonists had given up for England. They would have many more reasons to wonder about this in the second half of the 1700s.

Animals played an important part in colonial farm life. They provided food and were the main source of power on the farm. However, some animals were a constant problem for colonial farmers. These animals sometimes ate food meant for the farm family.

🐂 Oxen pulled plows and farm wagons. They were steady and reliable.

🐴 Horses were used to pull wagons and transpor people.

🦅 A scarecrow kept crows and other birds away from newly planted crops.

🐔 Chickens were found on most farms. They laid eggs and often wound up in a pot for Sunday dinner.

🐄 Every farmer needed a dairy cow to provide milk and cheese.

66

Animals

> Crows were everywhere in colonial America. Flocks of crows swept down on cornfields and ate the newly planted seeds.

Herds of sheep were common on colonial farms. Their wool was spun into thread and yarn. They also provided meat to eat.

Hogs not only provided ham and bacon, they were farm garbage disposals. They ate just about anything the farmers gave them.

Rats and mice invaded corn and other grains stored for the winter. The best defense against these rodents was a big barn cat.

CHAPTER FIVE

The Seeds of Revolution

****

Colonies Connected

The American colonies had made great progress by 1750. They had begun as a scattering of settlements surrounded by wilderness. By the middle of the 1700s, the settlements had become thirteen colonies with thriving cities, strong businesses, and farms that provided all the food the colonists needed. The colonies also grew and harvested plants, such as cotton and trees, that they could sell to Europe and the West Indies. Such products were called **cash crops**.

Roads now connected towns and cities from one colony to the next. Many of the roads were strewn with ruts and rocks, and they turned to mud with each heavy rain. Still, people could travel in just days between the major cities of

Colonial roads were little more than dirt tracks just wide enough for a horse or horse-drawn wagon.

Boston, New York City, Philadelphia, and Charles Town, South Carolina. They had horses and coaches to carry them. All along the roads, they would find taverns and inns where they could have a bed for the night and feed for the horses.

With easier travel came the ability to communicate more quickly from one colony to the next. The colonists had plenty of reason to be in touch with one another. The contest between England and France over American territory was not finished. War was about to strike America once again.

The French and Indian War

In 1754, a young officer named George Washington attacked a company of French soldiers in western Pennsylvania with a company of the Virginia militia. In the process, his troops killed at least a dozen French soldiers, including their commander. Washington and his troops were later attacked by a larger French force and had to surrender. Washington was sent back to Virginia with a message for the English governor. If the English returned to western Pennsylvania, it would mean war between France and England.

As it turned out, this attack against the French did set off the last war between France and England for possession of North America. The seven-year-long conflict became known as the French and Indian War.

Lieutenant Colonel George Washington led troops into battle against the French at the start of the French and Indian War.

In early spring of 1755, Governor William Shirley sent troops to Acadia in New France. French people had lived there for many years. British and American troops forced the Acadians to leave their homes. Many were sent to the colonies, while others escaped into the forests of New France. Shirley's troops claimed Acadia for England.

England formally declared war in 1756. From that time until 1759, colonial militias joined with British troops to drive the French out of North America once and for all. In the end, they succeeded. The Treaty of Paris, signed by the French and English governments in 1763, gave all of France's claims in North America to England.

The soldiers of New England learned a lot about the British troops as they fought beside them. The British were well trained and their camps were clean and tidy. They showed courage in the heat of battle, facing gunfire without running or hiding.

However, the British officers punished their own soldiers for breaking the slightest rule. The punishments were cruel beatings with a whip. The British soldiers also used bad language and forgot the Sabbath. They thought the colonists made poor soldiers. The colonists, on the other hand, thought the British were people who did not obey God.

Throughout the French and Indian War, people from the thirteen colonies came into regular contact with each other for the first time. Massachusetts soldiers fighting side by side with soldiers of other colonies realized that they all had a lot in common. The colonists began to realize that they were more American than they were British.

British troops along with colonial militia fought the French and their Indian allies for almost nine years during the French and Indian War.

Fire!

Many women became widows and their children became orphans when colonial soldiers died in the French and Indian War. By the war's end, one-third of the families in Boston had lost a loved father or son.

Yet life at home could be dangerous, too. Fire was a constant problem for Boston and other Massachusetts towns. Unlike a city such as Philadelphia, where many buildings were made of brick, Boston was built almost entirely of wood. Houses nestled close together on narrow, winding roads. As early as 1631, Boston's leaders had made wooden chimneys and thatched roofs illegal, because they went up in flames at the slightest spark. Even so, the city's buildings had to be rebuilt many times, because fires from fireplaces and candles were so hard to control.

As time passed and many more fires claimed lives and property, the city leaders realized they needed better equipment to fight fires. So Boston's leaders requested a fancy new engine from England. The engine was a wooden box 3 feet (0.9 meters) long and 18 inches (46 centimeters) wide, with handles for carrying it and a pump that pushed water through a small hose.

During a fire, a "bucket brigade" kept the box of the engine filled with water. To form the bucket brigade, people lined up in a double row. They passed buckets full of water down one row to the fire. Then they passed the empty buckets in the opposite direction along the other row to be refilled.

In 1678, the General Court of Massachusetts created the first engine company in colonial America. The court hired twelve men and a captain. Beginning in the 1700s, Boston also hired a "bellman." He worked from ten o'clock at night until five in the morning, watching for fires through the night. If he found a fire, he rang the church bells to alert the people that they were in danger and should come to help.

Firefighting Tools

By the 1760s, Boston firefighters had learned to always keep certain tools ready. Most important were the following.

A leather fire bucket Most households owned one of these buckets. Everyone who could lift a bucket needed to help in case of a fire. Leather was used because wooden buckets could burn more easily and metal buckets were harder to get.

A salvage bag Firefighters tried to save people's belongings in these bags. Things that had any value in a house were thrown into a salvage bag and carried or lowered to safety.

A bed key Often, a family's most valuable possession was a bed. The bed key was a small tool that allowed a firefighter to take a bed apart in a hurry so it could be saved from the fire.

By the 1760s, engines had become common. The *Boston Gazette* even carried advertisements for engines that could be kept at home. "Hand Engines made after the best manner…very useful in all families," one advertisement said. "Convenient for extinguishing fire in chimneys or in any room in a house…said engine throws water with ease 40 feet [12 meters] perpendicular."

Even so, in 1760, Boston suffered one of the worst fires in its history. Before the fire ended, 176 warehouses had burned down and many families had lost their homes. Then, in 1764, Harvard College burned down. As one witness reported, "It is [believed] to have begun in a beam under the hearth, in the Library where a fire had been kept."

Smallpox in the City

Just a month after Harvard burned, another danger struck. "Many persons in town," wrote one young man in February 1764, "have lately been visited with the smallpox, some of whom have died…. 'Tis now in 7 families." Smallpox had long since been one of the most dreaded diseases in the colonies. It began with a fever. Then a rash like chicken pox appeared. The rash caused sores containing pus to cover the skin. Many people died from the disease. People who survived were left with terrible scars from the sores.

A guide to the treatment of smallpox called "A Brief Rule" was published in 1677.

Smallpox spread quickly from person to person, so city leaders tried to separate those who came down with the disease from others. One way to do that was to send them to a "pesthouse." This was a hospital set aside for people with easily spread diseases. People often died in such places, however, so families of smallpox victims were likely to refuse this solution. In that case, leaders ordered that a flag be hung in front of a sick person's house. They also placed someone who had already survived the disease outside the door. This person, who could not get the disease again, would act as a guard to keep people from entering or leaving the infected household.

Sometimes, keeping people away from others did not work. In March 1764, smallpox spread throughout Boston. More than 1,500 Bostonians hurried away from the city to stay with friends and family in the country. Town leaders resorted to a risky solution to save those who remained.

Years before, doctors had found a way to help more people survive the disease. The solution was **inoculation**. Doctors gave people what they hoped would be a mild case of the disease on purpose. They took pus from the sores of people with mild smallpox and, using a needle, put it under the skin of healthy people. This gave them a mild case of the disease. If they survived, then they became immune to smallpox. This means they could never get the disease again. The danger of inoculation was that sometimes it gave people a bad enough case of the disease to kill them. Even so, more people who had been inoculated survived than those who had not gotten the treatment.

Boston's doctors got busy inoculating as many people as they could. About 5,000 people were inoculated. Only 46 of them died. Of the 700 people who caught the disease without inoculation, 124 died.

Time Together

Life in colonial Massachusetts was not all war and disease. In the many years since the colony had been founded, people had left behind many of the Puritans' strict ideas about fun. In the city, men gathered at the local coffee-houses or taverns to talk about politics or business and play billiards (also known as "pool" in later times). When women got together, they worked on quilts, shucked corn, or sewed. Once children had done their share of the chores and had completed their school lessons, they hurried outside to find playmates.

The colonists in town and country alike made the meetinghouse a central gathering place. The Puritan ministers preached sermons morning and afternoon on the Sabbath. Between the services, town families often met in each other's homes. For people who had traveled a distance to a meetinghouse, a special hall, a school, or even a tavern was set aside for them to wait for the afternoon service. Such places were called "noon houses" or Sabbath houses. Here, the country folk saw friends and ate together. In winter, they could warm themselves at the fire and put fresh, warm coals in the foot warmers they carried to the meetinghouse.

Puritan ministers preached long sermons to their congregations on the Sabbath.

During the week, the colonists used meetinghouses for local business. They met to elect officials, to vote on new schoolmasters, or to decide on the use of public land. Even these gatherings gave people a chance to socialize.

Playing cards became a favorite pastime, as did bowling on the green and shuffleboard. The Massachusetts folks never played for long, though. A little fun, and then it was back to the serious business of everyday life.

Fun and Games

Colonial children enjoyed many activities that children still enjoy today. They played tag and cat's cradle. They flew kites, ice-skated, and went swimming and fishing. They played many games with balls, marbles, and hoops. They even played badminton, only they called it "battledore and shuttlecock." Boys were given jackknives to use for carving, and girls received dolls and doll furniture.

On the same day in 1721 that the *Boston Gazette* advertised a horserace for adults, it offered something just for the boys. "There will be a pig run for boys at 9 in the morning," it said. "The boy who takes the pig and fairly holds it by the tail wins the prize."

Serious Business

Between 1764 and 1774, England's government passed a number of new laws and taxes. Parliament decided that the colonies should be giving England some of its profits. England had spent a lot of money protecting the English colonies in the French and Indian War. England now wanted to make the colonies pay back those expenses.

The Sugar Act of 1764 placed taxes on the colonies' trade with the West Indies and tried to stop the colonists' smuggling of sugar and molasses. In 1765, the Stamp Act taxed every piece of official paper used in the colonies. People had to pay for a stamp on newspapers, diplomas, land deeds, wills, and even tax receipts.

The Stamp Act required almost every type of paper document to carry a government stamp. Colonists had to pay for the stamps before they could buy paper products.

Massachusetts Bay and other colonies created a storm of protest. Acting together, the colonies declared that they should not have to pay a tax they had not agreed to pay. To show their anger, they boycotted all British imported goods. This meant that they refused to buy anything from England. They also formed an association called the Sons of Liberty. This group had members in many colonies. If England used its troops to make people obey the Stamp Act, the Sons of Liberty intended to raise an army of its own to fight back.

In Boston, a crowd of rioters created a life-size, stuffed doll (called an effigy) meant to look like the royal stamp distributor, Andrew Oliver. All day, on August 14, 1765, they left the effigy hanging from a tree. At the end of the day, they took the effigy down and paraded it through the streets. Finally, they took it to the city docks, where Oliver had his office. The mob destroyed Oliver's office and burned the effigy in a bonfire. As a result of these actions, the Stamp Act was **repealed** in 1766.

The next year, Parliament passed the Townshend Acts. These acts placed taxes on imported goods such as lead, glass, paper, paint, and tea. Again, the colonies launched a boycott of British goods. In Boston, huge groups of people gathered in the streets to protest. The British responded by getting rid of all the taxes except the one on tea.

The Boston Massacre

Reports of rioting in Boston reached the ears of King George III of England. People in America were keeping the tax collectors from doing their job. Even worse, Bostonians were threatening these royal officials or even doing them physical harm. England decided to send British troops to keep the peace in Boston. The colonists called these troops redcoats, because they wore red uniforms.

On October 1, 1768, British soldiers made camp on the green in Boston. From the moment the troops arrived, the people of Boston made their anger known. Newspapers throughout the colonies reported one incident after another in which citizens and soldiers came into conflict. The soldiers often treated people with little respect. The towns-people responded by getting in the soldiers' way as they patrolled Boston's streets. There were even occasional fistfights when tempers got out of control.

Finally, the situation heated to boiling point. On the night of March 5, 1770, a group of angry Boston men and boys gathered on King Street. When some soldiers going off duty tried to pass, the Bostonians stood in the way. They jeered at the soldiers and pelted them with snowballs laced with rocks.

No one ever really knew who gave the soldiers the order to fire their guns. But fire they did, right

British troops shot eleven Patriots in the Boston Massacre.

into the crowd. Five people were killed and eleven were wounded.

The townspeople demanded that the troops be removed from town and sent to an island fort called Castle William in Boston Harbor. The governor of Massachusetts, Thomas Hutchinson, did as they asked. A British captain and eight of his men were charged with murder. The colony quieted down, but not for long.

CHAPTER SIX

The Road to Independence

****

The Tea Act

Even though the colonists quieted down after the trouble in Boston, many continued to boycott British tea. Many people began drinking "freedom tea," made from sassafras or other herbs, instead. Other colonists, however, bought tea in support of the British government. People noticed who supported the king and Parliament. These people came to be called Loyalists, or Tories. People who resisted the English were known as Patriots.

One of Boston's most fiery Patriots, Samuel Adams, made sure people knew what the Patriot cause was all about. He wrote that the colonists were being taxed without having their own representatives in Parliament to speak up for them.

Massachusetts Patriot Samuel Adams was a fiery speaker against British control of the colony.

Patriots at the Wheel

The Patriots' resistance to British taxes made life difficult for many families. Because of the colonists' boycott of British imports, the colonies had to produce more at home. Men, women, and children all helped to make the boycotts work. Women grew more of their own food in their kitchen gardens. They learned to brew herbal tea from local plants instead of buying the imported tea. They did without the manufactured cloth they would usually buy from England. Spinning and weaving their own cloth became a patriotic act. Women attending one political gathering on Boston Common (the city's green) demonstrated their patriotism by actually setting up their spinning wheels on the common.

Patriot women learned to spin cotton, wool, and flax into thread and yarn when they were young girls.

He reminded people that the king's appointed tax collectors were using their power to make money for themselves. Worse yet, he said, British laws made colonists little more than servants by ordering them to do things without giving them a say in how their government was run.

Adams believed that the colonies should be free from England's rule. He was determined to keep the people of

Massachusetts stirred up against the British government. In November 1772, he formed groups called committees of correspondence to carry every piece of news to every village in the colony. When Parliament passed the Tea Act in 1773, the people of Massachusetts knew about it right away.

The Tea Act was intended to help a British trading house, the East India Company. The company had 18 million pounds (8.2 million kilograms) of tea to sell that the colonial merchants had been boycotting. The Tea Act would allow the company to sell the tea at a lower price than that sold by other companies. The company would keep its profits. The British government thought the colonists would welcome the cheaper tea. The British could not have been more mistaken.

A Tea Party in Boston

The colonists immediately rebelled against the Tea Act. To them, it looked like a trick to get them to buy only British tea. The colonists did not intend to let the English government control their lives. In Philadelphia and New York, when the East India Company's ships arrived with the tea, city officials made them turn around without unloading.

In Boston, Loyalist governor Thomas Hutchinson would not allow the trading company's three tea ships to be forced out. But the local Patriots would not let the ships be unloaded. The ships lay at anchor in the harbor, full of tea.

About fifty members of Boston's Sons of Liberty took matters into their own hands. Late at night on December 16, 1773, they dressed as Mohawk Indians and boarded the ships. Without noise or trouble, the men tossed 340 chests of tea overboard. A cargo worth 10,000 British pounds sank to the bottom of the harbor. This action was called the Boston Tea Party.

Samuel Adams's cousin, John Adams, wrote of the Boston Tea Party, "There is a dignity, a majesty…in this last effort of the Patriots that I greatly admire." He was not alone. Most of Boston's Patriots were in favor of the Sons of Liberty's tea party.

Closing Boston Harbor

The leaders in England had quite a different view. They did not intend to let the colonists rebel in such a way. So in the spring of 1774, they passed a series of laws that the colonists called the Intolerable Acts.

One of these laws closed Boston Harbor until the city paid the East India Company for the tea that had been destroyed. Boston's businesses depended on the port's commerce. Without business, people would soon run out of money for food and other necessary items.

Members of the Sons of Liberty dressed as Indians and threw British tea into Boston Harbor in what became known as the Boston Tea Party.

Another law changed the Massachusetts government. Many officials would now be appointed by Parliament instead of being elected by the colonists. In addition, towns would be allowed to have only one meeting a year for governing themselves.

The acts also stated that British soldiers who had committed crimes against colonists would not be tried in America. Instead, they would be sent back to England for trial. This meant that they probably would not be punished.

Liberty Boys

Like their parents, children paid attention to the patriotic messages of people like Samuel Adams. In the winter of 1774, a group of Boston schoolboys found their sledding path ruined because a servant of a British officer had spread ashes on it. The boys decided to form a committee to speak to the officer. They explained about the path and demanded fair treatment. The officer heard them out and then ordered his servant to fix the sledding path. Upon hearing of the incident, General Gage declared, "It [is] impossible to beat the notion of Liberty out of the people, as it [is] rooted in them from their childhood."

Finally, the British army was given permission to demand food and housing within any of the towns throughout the colonies. The colonists might have to give up their homes or other private buildings on the whim of a British officer. The first place this would happen on a large scale was Boston. And just to make sure the laws were enforced, Parliament replaced Governor Hutchinson with a military commander named General Thomas Gage.

These laws took away rights that the colonists were supposed to have. Samuel Adams and others believed that taking away the colonists' rights was the first step to making slaves of the colonists.

People throughout the thirteen colonies came to Boston's aid. They sent bushels of flour, barrels of wheat, pigs, sheep, and money to the city by land. At the same time, word was sent out that each colony should choose people to represent it at a meeting, the First Continental Congress, to be held in Philadelphia. A silversmith named Paul Revere was the first to mount his horse and carry the message south to the other colonies.

The First Continental Congress

All the colonies except Georgia agreed to send delegates, or representatives, to the congress in Philadelphia. Massachusetts sent four men, including John Adams and Samuel Adams. The delegates would decide how they thought the colonies should respond to the British government. On September 5, 1774, the congress began its work.

Meanwhile, fifty Bostonians met the following day to create a document they called the Suffolk Resolves (named after the county in which Boston was located). The resolves said that Massachusetts should prepare its men to fight. They also called for all the colonies to refuse to buy any British goods.

Once again, Paul Revere got on his horse. This time, he rode to Philadelphia and presented the Suffolk Resolves to the Continental Congress. When the resolves were read aloud, the delegates burst out cheering and clapping. They took a vote on the document, and every delegate voted to approve it.

By the time the congress finished, the delegates had agreed that the colonies would not buy or consume British goods. They would also refuse to sell American goods to England. This boycott would continue until Parliament repealed, or ended, the Intolerable Acts. Before the delegates left Philadelphia, they agreed to meet again in the coming year.

The Shot Heard 'Round the World

When King George III was told what the colonies intended, he was glad. "The New England governments are in a state of rebellion," he said. "Blows must decide whether they are to be subject to this country or independent." In other words, the colonies had given the king an excuse for a fight. He expected England to win.

Meanwhile, association committees were formed in towns and villages all over the colonies. These committees were groups of local leaders who would be in charge of gathering weapons and food supplies. They would also make sure that each town had a group of men ready to fight.

Concord, in the Massachusetts Bay Colony, was one of the first towns to create its own militia.

Surgeons

During the Revolutionary War, each colonial company of troops had its own doctor. Soldiers who were wounded or sick would almost certainly die without a doctor's care. Some doctors were more skillful than others, but they all worked hard to save soldiers' lives.

Camp surgeons, as they were called, dealt with dirty conditions and a constant lack of medical supplies. Most of the diseases the soldiers caught, such as smallpox, dysentery, and fever, were caused by the lack of cleanliness.

Sometimes, a soldier's leg or arm was damaged beyond repair by enemy weapons. Then the surgeon would have to amputate, or cut it off, so it did not become infected and kill the soldier. Anesthesia (drugs that deaden pain and make the patient sleep) did not exist. The best the doctor could do for the pain was to give the soldier some rum or brandy to drink and a wooden stick to bite down on. Two men would hold the soldier down while the surgeon sawed off the damaged limb. A good doctor could finish the job in less than forty-five seconds. Even so, only one soldier out of three survived an amputation.

The militia included minutemen—soldiers who could be "ready in a minute." Massachusetts colonists had received plenty of practice in fighting. They had fought Native Americans who had tried to drive the settlers off traditional Indian lands. The colonists had also fought in the French and Indian War. The colony's minutemen were young and strong. Concord had a list of 400 local men who were trained to fight. One hundred of these men were minutemen.

On April 15, 1775, General Gage prepared a secret march to capture or destroy the colonists' military supplies at Concord. He also planned to arrest Samuel Adams and John Hancock. Hancock was another active Patriot and delegate to the Continental Congress.

Patriot Paul Revere rode from Boston to Lexington to warn Samuel Adams and John Hancock that British troops were coming to capture them.

Paul Revere and a few other Patriots found out about Gage's plans. Revere agreed to be a messenger. He went first to warn Adams and Hancock. Then the people of Concord were warned. Immediately, the men and boys of the town loaded up ox wagons and carts to move all the military supplies. They hid the supplies in other villages and in the outlying swamps and fields. The minutemen got word that they should be armed and ready to march at a moment's notice.

On April 19, about 700 redcoats arrived at Lexington, Massachusetts, on their way to Concord. There, they found the local militia lined up on the town green. Most members of the Lexington militia were farmers with little training. They included boys and old men. Seeing that they were greatly outnumbered, the colonists started to leave. But someone fired a shot. Immediately, the British soldiers fired their muskets at the militia. The British killed eight and wounded ten. Then they marched on to Concord.

Few of the military supplies were still in Concord by this time. The redcoats found and destroyed a couple of cannons and threw 500 cannonballs into a nearby pond. These would be fished out later by the colonists. Meanwhile, the British fought local militias once again and then turned to march back to Boston. They did not know that thousands of colonial militiamen had now hidden themselves behind rocks and trees all along the road.

The battle that followed was like none these British troops had ever fought. They were used to armies that faced each other on the field of battle. However, the colonists fought like the Native Americans who had sometimes attacked them. They fired on the British from their hidden positions. As the redcoats made their way back to Boston, another 900 British soldiers arrived to help them. At the end of the day, though, 73 redcoats had been killed. Another 192 had been wounded, and the colonists had captured 22. On the American side were 49 dead and 39 wounded. The Revolutionary War had begun.

The Battle of Bunker Hill

By nightfall after the battles in Lexington and Concord, the British in Boston could see the watch fires of colonial militias surrounding the city. Militiamen poured into the area from all over New England. They were determined to hold the British army captive in Boston without a source of supplies.

General Gage waited out the **siege** for two months, until three more British generals with 1,100 troops had arrived by sea to help him. Finally, he prepared to break free. The Americans, however, had found out what he was planning, and they were prepared. They marched 1,200 men to Breed's Hill, where they had a view of Boston. (Breed's Hill was near Bunker Hill, which gave the battle its name.)

Colonial soldiers waited for the British troops to march up Breed's Hill. The colonial commander shouted to them, "Don't fire until you see the whites of their eyes."

Through the night, 400 more soldiers joined them and dug in for a fight.

On the afternoon of June 17, the British forces marched against Breed's Hill. The colonial militia put up a good fight, twice driving back the British. Finally, the Americans ran low on ammunition. When the British charged with bayonets, the Patriot soldiers were forced to retreat. They left behind them 140 dead and 271 wounded. The British captured 30 others. The redcoats' victory ended with 226 British soldiers dead and another 828 wounded. Meanwhile, 16,000 colonial militiamen surrounded Boston, keeping Gage's troops trapped in Boston. The siege continued.

CHAPTER SEVEN

From Bay Colony to State

****

The Continental Army

Patriots spread the word about the battles at Lexington and Concord throughout the colonies. The colonies faced difficult decisions. When the Second Continental Congress gathered in Philadelphia on May 10, 1775, the delegates had to consider how they should plan for war.

One of their first acts was to answer a cry for help from Massachusetts. The colony asked that the congress send a military leader, who would lead the army of colonists who were holding the British under siege in Boston.

The congress voted to send supplies to the colonial militia, which was now called the Continental army. The congress also appointed George Washington as the army's

General George Washington took command of the Continental army at Cambridge, Massachusetts, in 1775.

commander in chief. It chose other officers to go with him to Boston, as well. The congress also gave Paul Revere the job of printing money. The new money would be used in place of British currency to pay the soldiers.

Boston's Release

Once in Massachusetts, Washington began recruiting more troops. He wanted to create an army that would be strong enough to face the British in Boston. He then moved his troops to Dorchester Heights, an area that overlooked Boston.

General Washington moved his troops to Dorchester Heights, overlooking Boston, and prepared for battle.

Soldier Food

Food supplies were always a worry for the Continental army. This account of a soldier's diet comes from *Private Yankee Doodle,* by Revolutionary soldier Joseph Plumb Martin. "When we engaged in the service," he wrote,

we were promised one pound of good and wholesome fresh or salt beef, or three fourths of a pound of good salt pork, a pound of good flour, soft or hard bread, a quart of salt to every hundred pounds of fresh beef, a quart of vinegar...a gill [5 ounces] of rum, brandy, or whiskey per day, some little soap and candles.... But...I have gone one, two, three, and even four days without a morsel [bite].

The British did not want to repeat their experience at Breed's Hill. They did not march out to meet Washington's troops. Instead, in March 1776, the British troops boarded their ships and prepared to sail out of Boston Harbor. They invited any of the Tories who had remained in Boston during the siege to leave with them. Rather than face the anger of the Patriots, 1,100 Tories chose to sail with the British army to Halifax in Canada.

As the redcoats and Tories were leaving Boston Harbor, Washington and his army were marching into the city by land. Right behind them came many Patriots who had fled the city during the siege. They returned to find what one witness called "a melancholy [sad] scene." Trees, fences, and many houses had been taken down and used for firewood.

Shops had been emptied of their goods and homes had been looted. Further, many of the Tories who left had been important to Boston. They were judges, lawyers, doctors, merchants, ministers, and tradesmen.

Within days, Washington departed with the army to march against the British in New York. It was now up to the Massachusetts Patriots they had left behind to defend their port and their land.

Independence Declared

Meanwhile, a year after the congress had gathered, it was still busy keeping the colonies working together. In May 1776, the delegates instructed each colony to set up a new government that could run without any British officials. All British meddling should be ignored. The new governments should operate "under the authority of the people."

By June 11, the congress had selected a committee of delegates to write a statement that declared the colonies' independence. Thomas Jefferson of Virginia wrote the document based on instructions from the committee. Then the congressional delegates made the changes they wanted. On July 4, 1776, they approved the Declaration of Independence.

The congress also made plans to have the Declaration of Independence printed and carried to each of the colonies.

Printed copies of the Declaration of Independence were sent to every colony so that people could read and understand the document.

John Hancock, president of the congress, said it was important "that the people may be universally informed." The people needed to understand that the Americans would no longer be colonists. They would be citizens of their own country, the United States of America.

When the news reached Massachusetts, all but the remaining Tories were overjoyed. Throughout the colony, ministers read the Declaration to their congregations from the pulpit. It was entered into town records so that church members' children and grandchildren could read it for years to come. Town meetings had once been held "in his Majesty's name." Now they were held "in the name of the government and people of Massachusetts Bay." James Warren, a Patriot, wrote to John Adams that "every one of us feels more important than ever. We now congratulate each other as free men."

Fighting for Freedom

When the British left Boston, the war left Massachusetts soil. But Massachusetts soldiers did not leave the war. Thousands of the colony's men left their farms and shops to fight with the Continental army and navy.

Among those who fought were many of Massachusetts's black Americans, both freemen and slaves. Some slaves fought for the British, because they were promised freedom after the war. Many more fought for the Americans, beginning at Lexington and continuing until the end of the war in Yorktown, Virginia. For a brief time, when Washington took command of the army in 1775, blacks lost the right to enlist. Slaveholders feared that slaves might try to escape while in the army. When new recruits became scarce, however, black Americans were once more welcomed into the army.

Gunpowder Needed

Soldiers cannot fight a war without the proper ammunition. The colonies had always imported most of their gunpowder from England. Now England was the enemy. Even as he was marching from Boston, George Washington declared that gunpowder supplies were dangerously low. "We have but 32 barrels," he wrote.

In January 1777, Paul Revere helped local Patriots in Canton, Massachusetts, build a powder mill. By September, they had produced 37,962 pounds of the black explosive. The powder was not very good. Still, the mill supplied most of the gunpowder used by Massachusetts troops until 1779. Production stopped when the Canton mill blew up.

Women played their part as well. Some women and children went to war with their men. As "camp followers," they received a small amount of pay to cook, do laundry, and help as nurses.

But battlefield life was hard, and most women stayed home. With the men gone, they took over the work of running farms, shops, printing presses, and taverns. One Massachusetts woman wrote, "I have to provide everything for my family, at a time when it is so difficult to provide anything." Sometimes, life became very lonely. "Every trouble, however trifling [small]," wrote a wife at home to her husband on the battlefield, "I feel with double weight in your absence."

During the Revolution, Patriot women fought to defend their homes and families from the British.

A small number of women did not wait at home or sit in camp doing laundry while the men fought. They wanted to fight, too. They disguised themselves as men and joined the Continental troops as soldiers. Some managed to hide their gender through the entire war.

Wartime in Massachusetts Bay

Although Massachusetts had few battles on its own soil, it paid a high price for freedom from England. Most ordinary people were heavily taxed to support the war. At the same time, tradesmen lost business. Farmers had fewer hands to work their fields. Families on small farms in the western parts of Massachusetts barely had enough to live.

A few people actually became rich during the war. Market farmers with large farms made a lot of money supplying the army with food. Many merchants became rich as well. After the British left Boston, the merchants were able to trade once more with the West Indies and Europe. In 1778, the French decided to help the American cause. When French officers arrived in Boston, they needed supplies for their navy. This created even more profit for those who had supplies to sell.

Becoming a State

The Second Continental Congress instructed the colonies to make new **constitutions** or charters in 1776. The people of Massachusetts at first rejected the idea. The colonists wanted to be sure a state constitution would give everyone equal say in how they would be governed. They wanted to have the right to accept or reject the constitution that was created.

Finally, in 1779, the people in Massachusetts voted for a special convention to draft a state constitution. This was America's first constitutional convention. The delegates to the convention gathered in Boston in September. Among them were many Revolutionary War leaders, including John Adams, Samuel Adams, and John Hancock. John Adams was chosen to write the document.

Adams made representation the most important part of the constitution. Every person in the government would have to speak for the people who elected him. The constitution also called for public support of education. This meant that tax money would be spent to run the schools. Public support would also be given to religion. Taxpayers could apply their taxes to the Protestant church of their choice. Massachusetts citizens would have a free press, freedom to hold meetings, and the right "to keep and bear arms [guns] for the common defense."

Once the convention had agreed on Adams's document in March 1780, the constitution was sent to the towns to ratify (approve) it. It took until October 1780 for all the towns to respond and their votes to be counted. The convention members added up the votes and declared the constitution accepted, even though it was a close vote. An election was called, and John Hancock was elected as the first governor of the Commonwealth of Massachusetts.

The constitution did not abolish, or end, slavery. However, a series of court cases involving the slave Quock Walker occurred in 1783. During these cases, Walker argued for his freedom based on the new constitution of the state. In the final judgment, William Cushing, the chief justice of the Massachusetts Supreme Court, ruled that slavery was unconstitutional in the state of Massachusetts. Quock Walker was a free man.

Becoming a Nation

In 1781, the new United States adopted the Articles of Confederation as a governing document. The articles said that individual states must join together in "Perpetual Union" as the American Confederation. The rights and privileges of free citizens in one state would apply throughout all the states. States would be allowed to freely trade with one another. The articles also guaranteed that only the national congress could determine war or peace.

Many leaders came to believe that the articles would not be strong enough to hold the states together. It was decided that a constitutional convention, like the one in Massachusetts, should be held to draft a new constitution for the entire nation. As before, each state sent delegates to Philadelphia. The Constitutional Convention started in May 1787.

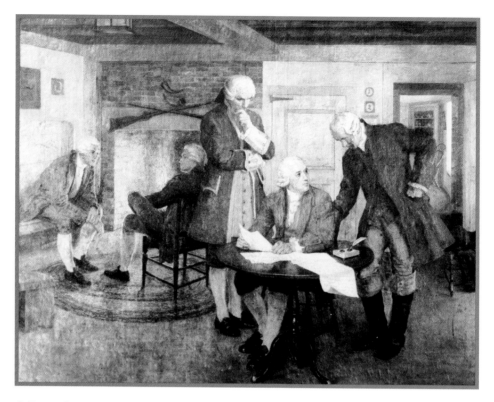

Massachusetts's delegates to the Constitutional Convention debated the new Constitution before signing the document and officially becoming part of the United States.

The delegates talked and argued about the Constitution throughout the summer of 1787. In September, when their discussions ended, the delegates signed the document. It was then sent to all of the states for ratification. Each state held a ratification convention of its own.

The Massachusetts convention met in early 1788. At first, a little more than half the delegates opposed the new federal (national) Constitution. They worried that a national government might not guard their liberties. They did not like the idea that officials could stay in office for more than one year. They also thought that the federal Constitution should provide public support for religion, as their own state constitution did.

The delegates in favor of the new Constitution finally persuaded some of the objectors to change their minds. On February 16, 1788, Massachusetts became the sixth state to ratify the U.S. Constitution.

In April 1789, George Washington began his job as the first president of the United States. At his side, as vice president, was John Adams of Massachusetts. They had important work to do as leaders of the new nation. The individual states still needed to learn how to work together as a single nation.

Thriving in a New Nation

Massachusetts came out of the Revolutionary War years with some battle scars. Yet the people began to prosper almost right away. Farms and businesses recovered. Merchants were able to increase their trade with Europe and the West Indies. They also opened new trade with ports in China and the Baltic region of northern Europe.

In 1796, George Washington announced that he would not serve as president again. John Adams was elected the second president of the United States, with Thomas Jefferson as his vice president. Adams continued to help the country put its new government into operation. He also worked to make the United States government strong enough to deal as an equal with the governments of other nations.

As the nation entered the 1800s, many Massachusetts citizens were still farmers. They carried fruit, vegetables, and grains to the cities of America's northeast to sell. They traveled in wagons, on horseback, or even on foot. In winter, farmers loaded butter and cheese onto horse-drawn sleighs to get their produce to market.

Massachusetts was also becoming a center of commerce and manufactured goods. In the towns and cities, new industries developed. Textile mills employed hundreds of people, including women and children. The state also became known for the fine furniture and musical instruments it produced. Its printers turned out newspapers, books, pamphlets, and magazines that were read throughout the United States.

A New Century

Boston continued to grow. By 1800, 25,000 people lived there. Many people living in the city had fancier homes and clothes than those in smaller towns and on farms. City people traveled to other cities by stagecoach. By the mid-1820s, more than 250 coaches left Boston every week, following 60 different routes.

Boston had a reputation as a clean city compared to others in the early 1800s. Unlike some American cities, Boston did not allow farm animals, such as pigs, to run free in the streets. Farmers collected horse manure from the city's roads to use on their fields. At night, workers drove horse-drawn carts through the city to clean out the privies (outhouses used as bathrooms) of the rich.

Massachusetts never lost its love of education. Public and private schools were offered to everyone. After 1790, dozens of private academies opened. These prepared students for a prosperous life and, in many cases, a college education at such schools as Harvard.

In many ways, Massachusetts would change in future years. Its people, however, remained as strong-minded and independent as the early Pilgrims and Puritans had been. The issues people argued about would shift over time. Massachusetts would later lead the nation in the fight to abolish slavery once and for all. The state would also take a strong stand on keeping people from drinking alcohol. Its citizens would insist on bettering the conditions of people working in factories. One  thing would remain the same. The people of Massachusetts would continue to fight for liberty and equality.

Recipe
Indian Pudding
and Nutmeg Cream

The Native Americans taught the colonists that cornmeal not only kept their bellies full, but also tasted good. The dish below would be eaten at any time of the day.

1/4 cup yellow cornmeal
1/4 teaspoon salt
3 cups milk
2 tablespoons butter
2 large eggs

1/2 cup molasses
2 tablespoons brown sugar, packed
2 tablespoons white sugar
1 teaspoon ground ginger

1/2 teaspoon ground cinnamon
1/3 cup dark raisins
2 cups light cream
1 teaspoon nutmeg

- Preheat an oven to 300° F. Butter an 8-inch baking dish.
- Combine the cornmeal and salt in a heavy saucepan.
- Gradually whisk in 2 1/2 cups of the milk.
- Whisk over medium heat until the mixture boils.
- Turn the heat to medium-low. Cook and stir until the mixture is thick and creamy (about 10 minutes). Remove from heat.
- Whisk the butter, eggs, molasses, brown sugar, white sugar, ginger, and cinnamon in a large bowl.
- Gradually whisk in the hot cornmeal mixture.

- Add raisins and stir. Pour the mixture into the baking dish.
- Pour the rest of the milk over the top of the pudding, but do not mix it in.
- Place the pudding dish into a larger baking dish. Pour enough hot water in the larger dish to come halfway up the sides of the pudding dish.
- Bake for 1 1/2 hours. Remove from the oven.
- Remove the pudding dish from the larger dish. Cool for 20 minutes.
- Mix cream and nutmeg. Spoon pudding into serving dishes. Top with cream.

This activity should be done with adult supervision.

Activity
Political Cartoons

The first cartoons to appear in American newspapers had political themes. In May 1754, the *Pennsylvania Gazette* published a newspaper article by Benjamin Franklin. Franklin wanted the colonies to unite. To make his point, he drew a picture of a snake cut into parts. The snake represented the divided colonies. This image became very popular in America during the Revolutionary War. It was printed in many newspapers and pamphlets. The picture made his point even more than his words.

You can create your own political cartoon that shows an issue facing the colonists or an issue facing your school or community. Maybe it will become as popular as Franklin's snake.

Procedure

Paper • Pencils or charcoal

- Pick a subject such as the environment, an election, or school safety that is easily symbolized in cartoon-style art.
- Draw a picture and add appropriately humorous text.

- Early editors and political cartoonists used many symbols in their artwork to represent issues. Make sure you use symbols that match your theme.
- Remember that the style of art in the earliest political cartoons was quite different from that found in today's newspapers. Use modern cartoon art or an old-fashioned style.

MASSACHUSETTS
Time Line

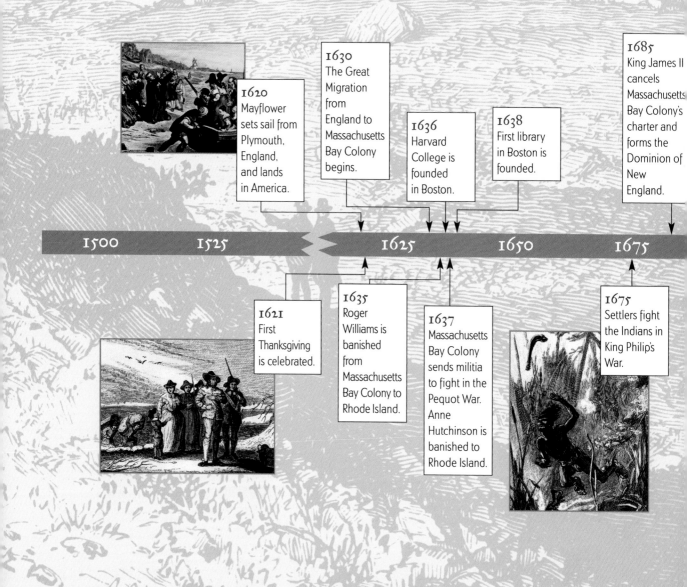

1620
Mayflower sets sail from Plymouth, England, and lands in America.

1630
The Great Migration from England to Massachusetts Bay Colony begins.

1636
Harvard College is founded in Boston.

1638
First library in Boston is founded.

1685
King James II cancels Massachusetts Bay Colony's charter and forms the Dominion of New England.

1500   1525   1625   1650   1675

1621
First Thanksgiving is celebrated.

1635
Roger Williams is banished from Massachusetts Bay Colony to Rhode Island.

1637
Massachusetts Bay Colony sends militia to fight in the Pequot War. Anne Hutchinson is banished to Rhode Island.

1675
Settlers fight the Indians in King Philip's War.

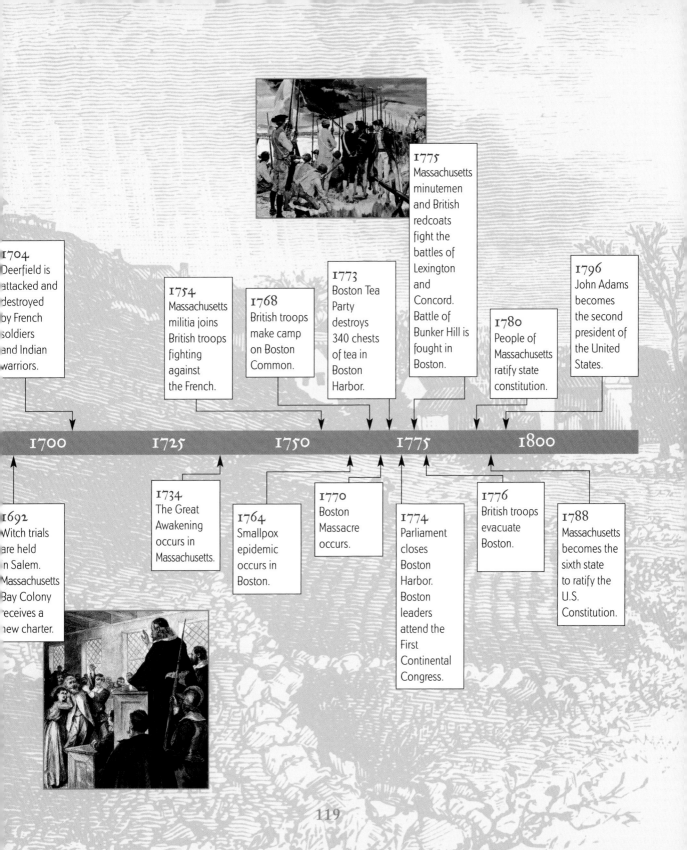

1704
Deerfield is attacked and destroyed by French soldiers and Indian warriors.

1754
Massachusetts militia joins British troops fighting against the French.

1768
British troops make camp on Boston Common.

1773
Boston Tea Party destroys 340 chests of tea in Boston Harbor.

1775
Massachusetts minutemen and British redcoats fight the battles of Lexington and Concord. Battle of Bunker Hill is fought in Boston.

1780
People of Massachusetts ratify state constitution.

1796
John Adams becomes the second president of the United States.

1700   1725   1750   1775   1800

1692
Witch trials are held in Salem. Massachusetts Bay Colony receives a new charter.

1734
The Great Awakening occurs in Massachusetts.

1764
Smallpox epidemic occurs in Boston.

1770
Boston Massacre occurs.

1774
Parliament closes Boston Harbor. Boston leaders attend the First Continental Congress.

1776
British troops evacuate Boston.

1788
Massachusetts becomes the sixth state to ratify the U.S. Constitution.

119

Further Reading

****

Barrett, Tracy. *Growing Up in Colonial America.* Brookfield, CT: Millbrook Press, 1995.

Curtis, Alice Turner, and Wuanita Smith. *A Little Maid of Massachusetts Colony.* Bedford, MA: Applewood Books, 1997.

King, David C., and Cheryl Kirk Noll. *Colonial Days: Discover the Past with Fun Projects, Games, Activities, and Recipes.* New York, NY: John Wiley, 1997.

Knight, James E. *Boston Tea Party.* Mahwah, NJ: Troll Associates, 1998.

Moore, Kay and Daniel O'Leary. *If You Lived at the Time of the American Revolution.* New York, NY: Scholastic, 1992.

Waters, Kate and Russ Kendall. *Tapenum's Day: A Wampanoag Indian Boy in Pilgrim Times.* New York, NY: Scholastic, 1996.

Ziner, Feenie. *Squanto.* North Haven, CT: Shoe String Press, 1988.

Glossary

****

abundance large quantity of something

ally people who support and help each other

breechclout also called a loincloth, a cloth worn around the waist by Indian men in warm weather

cash crop any crop grown in enough quantity to sell or barter for profit

charter an official, written document from a king or government that guarantees someone certain rights or privileges

condemn to place blame

constitution a set of laws that is used as the legal standard for a state or country

deputy a person appointed to be an assistant to or substitute for a leader, with the power to make official decisions

green grassy area that was often used for public meetings

hubbub excitement

import to bring an item from one country in order to sell it in another

innoculation medicine given through injection to prevent disease

militia men and boys who were not regular soldiers but were trained to fight and could be called to battle in case of attack by an enemy

profit money made in a business deal

prosperity success, wealth

repeal to officially revoke or stop an existing law

ritual a ceremony or practice repeated often as part of a tradition

sermon a talk that is part of a religious service

siege military action in which an area is surrounded

submerge to put something under water

thatch to make a roof of straw or other plant material

thimble a cover used when sewing to protect a finger from sharp needles

Index

✳✳✳✳✳✳✳✳✳✳✳✳✳✳✳✳✳✳✳✳✳✳✳✳✳✳✳✳✳✳✳✳✳